This Journal Belongs to :

Made in the USA
Monee, IL
22 December 2023

50379558R00057